MW00719205

Stepping Stones through
PILGRIM'S PROGRESS

The City of Destruction to the Cross

WRITTEN BY
C.J. LOVIK

INSPIRED BY
JOHN BUNYAN

FOREWORD

The extraordinary evangelical force of the original work by Bunyan has been largely lost on 21st century Christians living in the Post-Christian age. *The Sojourner's Adventure through Pilgrim's Progress* was written in order to remind Christians of the glorious fundamentals of our faith and to re-ignite the evangelical outreach that has, up until now, been the natural outcome of reading *The Pilgrim's Progress*.

This thumbnail sketch, titled *Stepping Stones through Pilgrim's Progress* is offered as both a preview of *The Sojourner's Adventure through Pilgrim's Progress*, and also a Gospel presentation.

I pray that it is a blessing to you and all who come in contact with the deep biblical truths found herein.

See you in the Celestial City!

C.J. Lovik
Lighthouse Gospel Beacon

Do the clamoring distractions of this world keep you from giving God a quiet moment in order to consider…

Where You Will Spend Eternity?

As I walked through the wilderness of this world, I came to a quiet place where I lay down. I soon fell asleep, and as I slept I dreamed a dream.

The truths in this thumbnail sketch of the famous book Pilgrim's Progress are presented to the reader as an allegory.

Isaiah 64:6a

But we are all as an unclean thing, and **All Our Righteousness Are As Filthy Rags...**

3

In my dream I saw a man named Graceless clothed in rags with a great burden on his back, holding a great book in his hands while standing outside the City of Destruction.

Romans 3:23
For All Have Sinned,
and come short of the glory
of God...

5

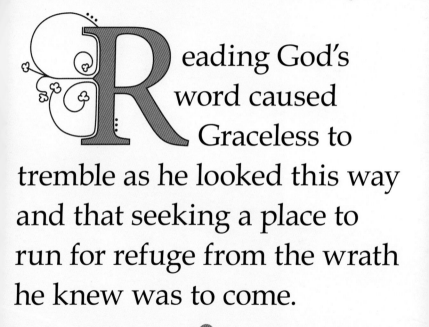

eading God's word caused Graceless to tremble as he looked this way and that seeking a place to run for refuge from the wrath he knew was to come.

Often loved ones, who are not in Christ, have little sympathy for the soul that has been awakened to its desperate need for forgiveness and deliverance.

Graceless, not knowing which way to flee, returns home to share his concern with his wife and family. They are concerned, but not because they believe what Graceless is telling them about the wrath to come, but rather because they think he is not in his right mind.

Acts 16:30

And brought them out, and said, Sirs, **what must I do to be saved?**

After a sleepless night, Graceless returns to the field outside the City of Destruction where he weeps and prays for help. Exhausted, he falls down on his knees and asks *What Must I Do To Be Saved?*

Is there a more important question we can ask as we take our brief pilgrimage through this world?

Hebrews 9:27

And as it is appointed unto men once to die, **but after this the judgment...**

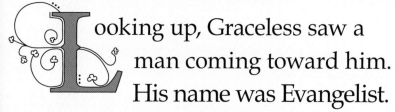

ooking up, Graceless saw a man coming toward him. His name was Evangelist. Evangelist raised Graceless to his feet and asked, "Why are you crying out?" Graceless answered, "Because I read in this book that I am condemned to die, and after that the judgment."

Hebrews 2:3a
How shall we escape,
if we neglect so great salvation...

13

Evangelist asks Graceless, "Do you see yonder small Sheep Gate?" Graceless answers "no." "Do you see yonder shining light?" Graceless answers, "I think so." Evangelist commands Graceless, "Keep that Light in your Eye."

The yonder Sheep Gate is the Good News regarding the death, burial and resurrection of Jesus the Christ. The Light is the Word of God that Evangelist commands Graceless to keep reading. The Light will lead to the small Sheep Gate.

Luke 14:26

If any man come to me, and hate not his father, and mother, and wife, and children, and brethren, and sisters, yea, and his own life also, he cannot be my disciple.

Without any prompting, Graceless makes a mad dash toward the shining light (reading God's Word). He believes that it will result in him coming to and entering into the small Sheep Gate where he will find deliverance from the wrath of God.

The small Sheep Gate is a picture of Jesus the Christ. Jesus Christ is the only way anyone will enter into eternal life.

Luke 17:32
Remember Lot's wife!

wo men decided to run after Graceless in order to persuade Graceless to return to the City of Destruction. Their names were Obstinate and Pliable. Instead of persuading Graceless, Obstinate returned to the city in a huff. Pliable, intrigued by the description of the Celestial City, decided to join Graceless on his pilgrimage.

2 Corinthians 4:18

While we look not at the things which are seen, but at the things which are not seen: for the things which are seen are temporal; **but the things which are not seen are eternal.**

19

liable is ravished as Graceless describes the forever kingdom and the eternal life guaranteed to all that reside within the Celestial City. "Let's hasten our pace!" Pliable pleads. "I cannot go any faster because of this great burden on my back," reports Graceless. Pliable has no burden and no interest in reading the Great Book.

1 John 2:19a

They went out from us, but they were not of us...

Now I saw in my dream that there was a swamp in the middle of the valley. Not paying attention, both Graceless and Pliable sunk into the swamp. Pliable quickly got out on the side nearest the City of Destruction and cursed Graceless for persuading him to come on a journey that was so fraught with danger. Graceless struggled to get to the other side but was unable to lift himself out of the swamp.

Psalm 40:2

He brought me up
also out of an horrible pit,
out of the miry clay, and set my feet
upon a rock, and established my goings.

23

G raceless lay exhausted and unable to move. Suddenly he heard a voice, "Give me your hand." Graceless lifted his arm and a moment later found himself on solid ground looking up at the face of a stout robust man whose name was, Help.

24

The Swamp that Graceless found himself mired in is called the Swamp of Despair and it is a picture of all the doubts and unbelief that all the enemies of the Son of God use to discourage pilgrims from coming to Him in faith, believing.

Romans 3:28

Therefore we conclude that a man is justified by faith without the deeds of the law.

Once Graceless is on his feet he brushes himself off, thanks Help and continues on the path that leads to the small Sheep Gate. He has not gone very far before his journey is interrupted by a man named Mr. Worldly Wiseman, who mock Graceless for seeking relief in Christ alone.

Mr. Worldly Wiseman is a picture of the liberal ministers who mock the truth that we can find relief in Christ alone by faith alone.

1 Corinthians 1:18

For the preaching of the cross is to them that perish foolishness; but unto us which are saved it is the power of God.

Galatians 3:10

For as many as are of the works of the law are under the curse: for it is written, Cursed is every one that continueth not in all things which are written in the book of the law to do them.

Hebrews 12:21

And so terrible was the sight, that Moses said, I exceedingly fear and quake.

29

Galatians 3:11-13

But that no man is justified by the law
in the sight of God, it is evident: for,
The just shall live by faith.
And the law is not of faith: but,
The man that doeth them
shall live in them.
**Christ hath redeemed us from
the curse of the law...**

Hebrews 10:38

Now the just shall live by faith:
but if any man draw back,
my soul shall have no pleasure in him.

Persuaded by the smooth words of Mr. Worldly Wiseman, Graceless tries to make his way to the home of Mr. Legality in order to have his burden removed. On the way he finds himself paralyzed with fear under Mount Sinai. Evangelist comes to his rescue.

How many pilgrimages that might have ended in true salvation have been hijacked by the lie that God will be pleased with our "good works" and the keeping of the law?

Matthew 7:13

Enter ye in at the strait gate: for wide is the gate, and broad is the way, that leadeth to destruction, and many there be which go in thereat...

Evangelist scolds Graceless for departing from the true way and tells him that there are three things that Mr. Worldy Wiseman said that he must abhor.

1. He turned you out of the true and only Way.
2. He mocked the cross and tried to make it odious to you.
3. He put you on a path that leads to everlasting destruction.

Matthew 7:7
Ask, and it shall be given you; seek, and ye shall find; **knock, and it shall be opened unto you...**

Like a man fleeing a burning building, Graceless makes his way without delay to the small Sheep Gate. He knocks and knocks and finally is greeted by Goodwill who asks who he is, where he came from and why he wishes to enter.

Goodwill represents God's good will toward repentant sinners. When asked why he should be allowed to enter, Graceless answers with the only truth that will open the door. He is a sorry sinner, and undeserving rebel that has put his faith and trust in the King's Son, the Lord Jesus Christ, who shed His precious blood in order that sinners might be reconciled to God the Father.

John 6:37

All that the Father giveth me shall come to me; and him that cometh to me I will in no wise cast out.

Graceless pleads with Goodwill to grant him entry. Goodwill asks who he is, where he came from and why he should be allowed to enter. Graceless replies, "I am a poor burdened sinner, I come from the City of Destruction but I am going to Mount Zion in order that I might be delivered from the wrath to come. I have put my life in the hands of the King's Son who died that I might live!"

Ephesians 6:16

Above all, taking the shield of faith, wherewith ye shall be able to quench all the fiery darts of the wicked.

Goodwill tells Graceless that he is willing with all his heart to grant him entry, and with that said, he grabbed ahold of Graceless and pulled him in with such force that Graceless, once inside the gate, tumbled to the ground. "I would have entered willingly," protested Graceless. Goodwill smiled, picked him up and took him to the little window and bid him look out and to the left.

Ephesians 6:12

For we wrestle not against flesh and blood, but against principalities, against powers, against the rulers of the darkness of this world, against spiritual wickedness in high places.

Peering out the little window, Graceless saw a strong castle, of which Satan is the captain. From there he, and those that serve him, shoot arrows at those who come up to the small Sheep Gate in order to kill or wound any pilgrim before they enter into the gate, which is a picture of Christ alone.

Ephesians 2:4-5
But God, who is rich in mercy,
for his great love wherewith he loved us,
Even when we were dead in sins,
hath quickened us together with Christ,
by grace ye are saved...

43

You now have a new name my child. From this moment on your name is no longer Graceless Fit for Wrath but **Christian Fit for Glory.**" At this, Christian blushed with excitement as the tears streamed down his face. Goodwill continued, "You are sealed with a promise that cannot be broken." Christian asked, "A promise that I will have a safe journey to the Celestial City?" "No indeed," replied Goodwill. "The promise that you now have Eternal Life and nothing can change that fact."

John 15:26
But when the **Comforter** is come, whom I will send unto you from the Father, even the Spirit of truth, which proceedeth from the Father, he shall testify of me...

Goodwill puts Christian on the path to life. The Straight Way. He tells Christian to go to the House of the Interpreter which is a picture of the Holy Spirit. It is there that Christian will receive further guidance and instruction that will help and comfort him on his journey to the Celestial City.

46

The sweeping that just makes things noxious is a picture of the LAW. The water sprinkling and cleaning is a picture of sin that is vanquished and the soul made spotless through the only one who perfectly kept the law, Jesus Christ.

Christian knocks on the door of the House of the Interpreter and is invited in where he is taken to a room that is being swept. The more the room is swept the harder it is to breathe through all the dirt and dust. After the dust settles it is sprinkled with water and wiped clean.

James 2:10
For whosoever shall keep the whole law, and yet offend in one point, he is guilty of all.

Passion is a picture of the men of this world who want it all now while Patience is a picture of the men of the world to come that is both gloriously superior and everlasting.

The Interpreter takes Christian into a room where there are two children. One is named PATIENCE and the other PASSION. Passion wants his treasure now and so he is granted the desires of his heart. The things he receives do not last but are temporal. Patience is willing to wait for the things he desires for they are both better and everlasting.

And so, after he had **patiently** endured, he obtained the promise.

Hebrews 6:15

Christian wonders how the Grace of God is maintained in the soul despite all the attempts of the enemy to extinguish it.

51

Viewing the fire in the fireplace that cannot be put out no matter how much water is thrown on it puzzles Christian.

Romans 8:38

For I am persuaded, that neither death, nor life, nor angels, nor principalities, nor powers, nor things present, nor things to come...

The mystery is solved!

The Interpreter (Holy Spirit) leads Christian to the other side of the fireplace where he discovers the solution to the mystery. Christ Himself maintains the work.

Nor height, nor depth, nor any other creature, shall be able to separate us from the love of God, which is in Christ Jesus our Lord.

Romans 8:39

John 14:26

But the **Comforter,** which is the Holy Ghost, whom the Father will send in my name, he shall teach you all things, and bring all things to your remembrance, whatsoever I have said unto you.

hristian is shown many other mysteries that are included in the original expanded version of *The Sojourner's Adventure through Pilgrim's Progress.* The Interpreter points Christian to the path which leads to the final destination that concludes this thumbnail sketch of Pilgrim's Progress. Where do you suppose that is?

1 Corinthians 1:18

For the preaching of the **cross** is to them that perish foolishness; but unto us which are saved it is the power of God.

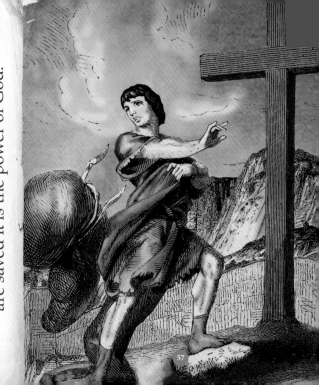

57

Christian follows the directions given to him at the House of the Interpreter. He soon comes to a path that leads him up a small hill. Suddenly he sees the Cross atop the hill and begins to weep with joy at the very sight of it. At that very moment his burden falls off his back and tumbles down the hill, never to be seen again.

THE END

Looking unto Jesus the author and finisher of our faith; who for the joy that was set before him endured the **cross**...

Hebrew 12:2a

It is very important for the reader to understand that at least 7 things happen the moment a sinner comes to Christ in faith, believing.

1. Your sins are forgiven and you now have Peace with God.
2. You are stripped of your rags and clothed with the Righteousness of Christ.
3. You are given an indelible mark that seals you as one of God's children forever.
4. You are given a hunger for the truth that can only be satisfied by reading God's word which produces a sensible assurance of salvation.
5. You are indwelt by the Holy Spirit who leads you into truth and when not quenched produces the blessed hope of Christ's return and the anticipation of a heavenly home.
6. You are vexed by your flesh that wars against the spirit and look forward to receiving a glorified body that cannot and will not ever sin again.
7. You are instilled with a love for God the Father as you lose your love for this present world.

Dear Reader,

Although there may be many steps or few that lead a sinner to the cross of Christ, personal salvation is not a process that takes place over time.

Although we must not forget that the Cross event has an eternal time-frame from God's perspective. This truth was revealed in the Book of Revelation, the last book in the Bible that records the testimony of Jesus Christ Himself. Read what it says:

Revelation 13:8
And all that dwell upon the earth shall worship him, whose names are not written in the book of life of the Lamb slain from the foundation of the world.

For us who are living on the earth, salvation is an instantaneous supernatural event that happens the moment we come to Christ in faith believing in His death, burial and resurrection. Saving faith is non-meritorious, unconditional and brimming over with gratitude as we receive the free gift of Christ's atonement personally.

Salvation by grace through faith is, however, a time-stamped offer that had a beginning nearly 2000 years ago, and will one day soon come to an end. For now, we can say with certainty that the offer has not expired. The day of salvation has not come to an end. We should rejoice in that simple fact. Today is the day of salvation.

2 Corinthians 6:2
For he saith, I have heard thee in a time accepted, and in the day of salvation have I succored thee: behold, now is the accepted time; behold, now is the day of salvation.

To be clear you must believe three fundamental facts about Jesus in order to be saved. **(1)** Jesus lived a perfect life, something none of us can do, **(2)** Jesus died on a wooden cross and was buried, and finally **(3)** Jesus rose from the dead on the third day after He was placed in the tomb.

The Apostle Paul made these simple historical facts crystal clear and tied them to the Gospel for all time and eternity.

1 Corinthians 15:1-4

Moreover, brethren, I declare unto you the gospel which I preached unto you, which also ye have received, and wherein ye stand;
By which also ye are saved, if ye keep in memory what I preached unto you, unless ye have believed in vain.

*For I delivered unto you first of all that which I also received,
how that Christ died for our sins according to the scriptures;
And that he was buried, and that he rose again
the third day according to the scriptures...*

This is the bedrock truth upon which the Good News about Jesus is indisputably founded. Without acknowledging these historical facts there is no sense going any further in your quest for truth. Without these three cornerstones firmly in place God cannot and will not save you. And to be clear, these are facts that Jesus Himself declared in advance to be both true and the touchstone for anyone who believed in Him.

John 3:16

*For God so loved the world, that he gave his only
begotten Son, that whosoever believeth in him should
not perish, but have everlasting life.*

The gift of salvation is based on something you had nothing to do with. It is based on the blood sacrifice of the only begotten Son of God, the only redemptive event that extinguishes God's righteous wrath.

Working this all out in order that you might be reconciled to God was not easy or cheap; it cost God a price that the entire sum total of all the wealth of all the nations over all generations of time could never pay.

1 Corinthians 6:20
*For ye are bought with a **price:** therefore glorify God in your body, and in your spirit, which are God's.*

Think about it. He sacrificed His only son, who willingly, and we are told joyfully, went to the cross, gave up His life (no one took it from Him) in order to pay the gross sin debt that we owed so that we might eternally and miraculously beyond reason dwell with Him forever and ever.

Hebrews 12:2

Looking unto Jesus the author and finisher of our faith; who for the joy that was set before him endured the cross, despising the shame, and is set down at the right hand of the throne of God.

If this was a debt you could pay with your own good works or good intentions, don't you think God would be happy to receive you based on your merits?

Of course, He would! He is merciful and He is also just.

The problem is that you and I, and every other living soul have hearts that, according to God, and borne out by both human history as a whole, and your history in particular, are desperately WICKED and constantly sinning in both thought and deed!

There are two kinds of people who don't dispute the historical record regarding Jesus but will never receive the free gift He offers.

The first kind is the person who thinks God weighs man's life in the balance and examines their deeds done during this brief space of time on this earth. If the good outweighs the bad then it would be unreasonable not to permit them into Heaven. Or so the logic goes.

Others believe God grades on the bell curve. The thinking goes like this: *I am not that bad. I have a good heart and cannot imagine that God would reject me. Those that are great sinners, yes, they might need special assistance. But I am basically good and deserving of God's approval.*

Since we are not the judge, and God is, perhaps we should see what He thinks. Fortunately, we do not have to guess what God thinks about all this, we have a written record of the Almighty's thoughts on this matter.

First, look at what God thinks as reported by the prophet Isaiah. And please notice God is not talking about our sin but our righteous acts, the very ones we think tip the scales in our favor.

Isaiah 64:6
But we are all as an unclean thing,
and all our righteousnesses are as filthy rags;
and we all do fade as a leaf; and our iniquities,
like the wind, have taken us away...

Now here are just few samples of what God declares about our sin problem.

Romans 3:23

For all have sinned, and come short of the glory of God...

1 John 1:10

*If we say that we have not sinned, we make him a liar,
and his word is not in us.*

Romans 5:12

*Wherefore, as by one-man sin entered into the world,
and death by sin; and so, death passed upon all men,
for that all have sinned...*

In other words, if you believe in Relative Righteousness—if you think that God is judging on the bell curve—you need to readjust your dangerously mistaken preconceptions and bring them in line with the revealed mind of God on the matter of sin.

In a nutshell, God says that the soul that sins will die. That includes you and me!

The other kind of person who does not dispute the recorded history about the life of Jesus but will never receive the free gift He offers is the person who thinks that God would never forgive their sins because their sins are too gross, too great and too many.

God has an argument with this person also. The crux of it is as follows. Looking at it from God's point of view it really is a compelling argument.

If you think you're too great a sinner to ever be forgiven you need to answer the following questions:

1. Do you really think so little of the precious blood of Jesus and the promises of God?

2. Where does the opinion about the inadequacy of the Cross of Christ come from? Not from Heaven that is for sure. Perhaps the other place?

3. Is your sin greater than God's **GRACE?**

Before we answer these questions let's take a look at an event that on its face argues against this low opinion of God's redemptive power and plan as fulfilled in the life, death, burial and resurrection of Jesus Christ.

Luke 23: 39-43

And one of the malefactors which were hanged railed on him, saying, If thou be Christ, save thyself and us. But the other answering rebuked him, saying, Dost not thou fear God, seeing thou art in the same condemnation?

> *And we indeed justly; for we receive the due reward of*
> *our deeds: but this man hath done nothing amiss.*
> *And he said unto Jesus, Lord, remember*
> *me when thou comest into thy kingdom.*
> *And Jesus said unto him, Verily I say unto thee,*
> *Today shalt thou be with me in paradise.*

Yet even with all the evidence God has laid before us to the contrary, many are invested in the fabricated notion that they are too great a sinner.

First let's look at what God reveals about the power of His Son's sacrifice.

Romans 5:8
But God commended his love toward us, in that, while
we were yet sinners, Christ died for us.

Romans 5:20
Moreover, the law entered, that the offence might abound. But where sin abounded, grace did much more abound...

Ephesians 2:1
And you hath he quickened, who were dead in trespasses and sins...

We could provide over 100 citations but let's just make the point with the testimony of one man. His name was Saul of Tarsus and he murdered and tormented Christians. Jesus saved him. You can read about this in the book of Acts. Listen to what Saul who became the Apostle Paul says:

1 Timothy 1:15
This is a faithful saying, and worthy of all acceptation, that Christ Jesus came into the world to save sinners;
of whom I am chief.

If you fall into either of these groups, if you think you are so good you don't need a savior or so bad He would never stoop to save you…think again!

You are invited to come empty handed to the Cross of Jesus Christ and with open eyes of faith, look up and see your savior.

It is really that simple for you.

Yes, it is true that there is one sin **God will never forgive.**

Do you know what sin that is?

It is called the unforgivable sin because it disqualifies you permanently from ever entering His presence with your sins forgiven.

What is the unforgivable sin?

Is it murder? King David murdered as have countless others who have been cleansed and forgiven.

Is it adultery? King David committed adultery as did countless others who have been cleansed by the blood of Jesus.

Is it lying? That would disqualify every single one of us and the offer of salvation would have never been made.

So, what is the unforgivable sin that we are told is a sin against the Holy Spirit? A sin so terrible that it disqualifies us from Heaven.

Is it blasphemy? Apparently not since the Apostle Paul was before his conversion the chief among the blasphemers of Christ.

The unforgivable Sin against the Holy Spirit of God is **Rejecting**

the free offer of Salvation made possible by the death, burial and resurrection of Jesus.

Remember that He died for all, but all will not receive the free gift. To reject God's plan to redeem mankind—a plan motivated by grace and mercy alone—is the ultimate slap in the face of God and the one act of pride and arrogance on the part of man that cannot be, and will not be forgiven.

The free offer of salvation remains for as long as you are alive, but once you die without receiving Christ your doom is sealed forever.

1 Corinthians 1:18

For the preaching of the cross is to them that perish foolishness; but unto us which are saved it is the power of God.

Hebrew 9:27

And as it is appointed unto men once to die, but after this the judgment...

If you want to guarantee that you will **NEVER** be reconciled to God, **NEVER** have your sins forgiven, and **NEVER** dwell with Him forever in a place so glorious and splendid that words fail, all you need to do is **REJECT CHRIST.**

It is the purpose of this little book to persuade you to receive the free gift of salvation before it is too late.

Now is the day of Salvation!

Ephesians 2:8-9

*For by grace are ye **saved** through faith; and that not of yourselves: it is the gift of God: Not of works, lest any man should boast.*

You may not have a tomorrow but even if you do, one day your life will be over and what will happen after that?

It is up to you to answer that question.

So, what must I do to be saved?

Romans 10:9
That if thou shalt confess with thy mouth the Lord Jesus, and shalt believe in thine heart that God hath raised him from the dead, thou shalt be saved.

Romans 10:13
For whosoever shall call upon the name of the Lord shall be saved.

You are either in Christ or you are an enemy of God. What will it be?

It is important to understand as you read the final pages in this little book that there is a space of time and events that happen between entering the small Sheep Gate which is Christ and Christian finally losing his burden at the cross.

Remember that this is an allegory and as such the literary elements of both allegory and time are used to unfold all the events that are actually included at the instant a person confesses with their mouth and believes in their heart that Jesus has died on the cross in order to wipe clean the debt of sin that they personally owe. That is the moment, with no time lapse, that the wrath of God is extinguished and we are covered with the righteousness of Christ forever.

So, as you read about the House of the Interpreter, a picture of the work the Holy Spirit does in the life of a believer as He takes up permanent residence in the heart, keep in mind that this happens the moment you come to Christ.

As you read about Christian losing his burden of sin and guilt at the cross, please understand that this also happens as a reality the moment a sinner trusts in Christ.

It may take years for a sinner to be fully sensible to that fact, but that does not change the reality of God's Word that informs us that the moment we believe, whether we are sensible to the miracle or not, we are saved.

Bunyan used an allegory to display the central truths about the gospel of Jesus Christ in a way that allows for a period of time to pass.

This is simply the consequence of the literary device used to proclaim the truth, not a reflection of the instantaneous reality of the new birth which happens the moment you trust in Christ alone as your Lord and Savior. Receive Him now, PLEASE!

John 1:11-12

He came unto his own,
and his own received him not.
But as many as received him,
to them gave the power to become
the sons of God, even to them
that believe on his name...

If you've called out to God and asked Him to redeem you, send us a message. We'd like to connect with you and send you some free resources which will help you on your journey.

If you'd like more information about becoming a Christian, or if you have questions, please reach out to us using the email below. We'd love to answer any questions you might have.

feedback@lighthouse.pub

www.lighthouse.pub